Weekly Reader Books presents

Checking 'Em Out & Sizing 'Em Up

A Children's Book about Opinions and Prejudice

by

Joy Wilt

Illustrated by Ernie Hergenroeder

Educational Products Division
Word, Incorporated
Waco, Texas

Author

JOY WILT is creator and director of Children's Ministries, an organization that provides resources "for people who care about children"—speakers, workshops, demonstrations, consulting services, and training institutes. A certified elementary school teacher, administrator, and early childhood specialist, Joy is also consultant to and professor in the master's degree program in children's ministries for Fuller Theological Seminary. Joy is a graduate of LaVerne College, LaVerne, California (B.A. in Biological Science), and Pacific Oaks College, Pasadena, California (M.A. in Human Development). She is author of three books, *Happily Ever After, An Uncomplicated Guide to Becoming a Superparent*, and *Taming the Big Bad Wolves*, as well as the popular *Can-Make-And-Do Books*. Joy's commitment "never to forget what it feels like to be a child" permeates the many innovative programs she has developed and her work as lecturer, consultant, writer, and—not least—mother of two children, Christopher and Lisa.

Artist

ERNIE HERGENROEDER is founder and owner of Hergie & Associates (a visual communications studio and advertising agency). With the establishment of this company in 1975, "Hergie" and his wife, Faith, settled in San Jose with their four children, Lynn, Kathy, Stephen, and Beth. Active in community and church affairs, Hergie is involved in presenting creative workshops for teachers, ministers, and others who wish to understand the techniques of communicating visually. He also lectures in high schools to encourage young artists toward a career in commercial art. Hergie serves as a consultant to organizations such as the Police Athletic League (PAL), Girl Scouts, and religious and secular corporations. His ultimate goal is to touch the hearts of kids (8 to 80) all over the world—visually!

This book is a presentation of Weekly Reader Books.
Weekly Reader Books offers book clubs for children from
preschool through junior high school.

For further information write to:
WEEKLY READER BOOKS
1250 Fairwood Ave.
Columbus, Ohio 43216

Checking 'Em Out and Sizing 'Em Up

This edition is published by arrangement with Educational Products Division, Word, Incorporated, 4800 West Waco Drive, Waco, Texas 76710.

ISBN: 0-8499-8142-5
Library of Congress Catalog Card Number: 79-53570

Joseph Paul, Editor

The educational concepts presented in the Ready-Set-Grow book series are also featured in a music songbook and longplay record. For further information concerning these materials see your local bookstore or write Word, Incorporated, 4800 West Waco Drive, Waco, Texas 76710.

4 5 / 84 83 82

This is because opinions are not built into a person's brain at birth. They are formed as a person grows up.

You form your opinions, but there are many things in your environment that affect the way you form them:

People, places, and experiences that surround you.

These things influence you to think the way you do. They are called environmental influences.

Environmental influences are all of the things around you that contribute to the opinions you form.

This is Rodney. Rodney has many opinions about many things. Rodney forms his own opinions, but there are many environmental influences that help persuade him to think the way he does.

People are environmental influences. This is Rodney's family—his parents, brothers, sisters, grandparents, uncles, aunts, and cousins.

These are Rodney's friends.

Rodney's family and his friends are both environmental influences that affect the way he thinks.

These are Rodney's enemies.

These are some other people that Rodney comes in contact with—his teacher, his coach, his doctor, his dentist, his minister, the clerk at the local grocery store, the saleslady at the toy store, his next door neighbor.

Rodney's enemies and all the other people he comes in contact with have an influence on the way he thinks.

Places are environmental influences. This is where Rodney lives.

Where Rodney lives is an environmental influence that affects the way he thinks.

This is where Rodney goes to school.

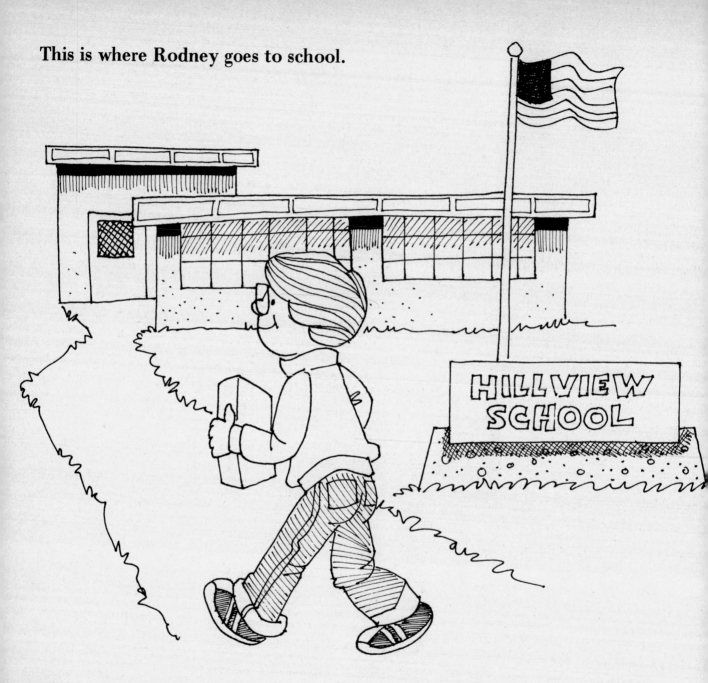

This is where Rodney goes to church.

Both Rodney's school and his church are environmental influences that affect the way he thinks.

41

This is the town where Rodney lives and goes to work.

He washes dishes and helps clean up at the El Taco Cafe.

Both the town and the place where Rodney works are environmental influences that affect the way he thinks.

Experiences are environmental influences. The things that Rodney sees on television or at the movies are environmental influences that affect the way he thinks.

The things that Rodney reads in books, magazines, and newspapers are also environmental influences.

The things that Rodney listens to on tape recordings, records and on the radio are environmental influences that affect the way he thinks.

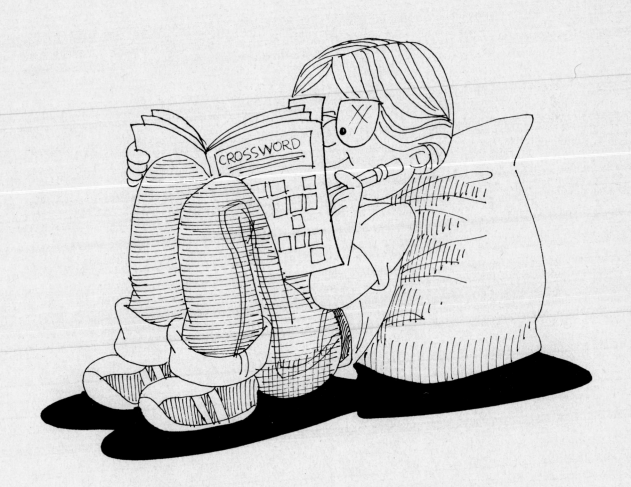

The things Rodney does are also environmental influences.

The things that happen to Rodney are environmental influences that affect the way Rodney thinks.

Your thinking, like Rodney's, is influenced by many things.

All the people, places, and experiences in your life are environmental influences that affect the way you think.

If it is true that your environmental influences affect your thinking and behavior, do you have any control over the way you think and act?

The next chapter will answer this question for you.

Chapter 3

Forming Your Own Opinions

You can control most of the information you receive from your environmental influences . . .

HEY, RODNEY! DID YOU KNOW THAT BOYS ARE NOT AS SMART AS GIRLS?

but you cannot control all of it completely.

53

The thing you can control completely is what you do with the information you receive from your environment.

The kinds of opinions that you form from the information you receive are up to you.

There are several things you need to do in order to form good opinions.

Step 1: Be aware of the information that you are receiving from your environmental influences.

For all the information you receive try to decide whether it is true or false.

Step 2:   Keep an open mind.

There are at least two sides to every issue. The information you receive from one environmental influence is only one side of the issue, and that one side may or may not be true.

One way to gather information is by talking with as many people as you can about the issue. As you talk with each person, try to figure out . . .

Why does this person feel the way he or she does?

What is his or her purpose for thinking the way he or she does?

In what way do you agree or disagree with the person, and why?

You can gather information by observing, experimenting, and doing research.

Read books, magazines, and newspapers that can give you information about the issue. Watch TV programs, and listen to radio programs about the issue. And don't stop observing, experimenting, and researching until you have all the information you need to form an intelligent opinion.

MY SISTER SAYS THAT "BOYS ARE NOT AS SMART AS GIRLS." MY TEACHER SAYS THAT "HOW SMART YOU ARE DOES NOT DEPEND ON WHETHER YOU ARE A BOY OR A GIRL." THE OTHER RESEARCH I'VE DONE SAYS THAT A PERSON'S INTELLIGENCE IS NOT DETERMINED BY HIS OR HER SEX... HMMM.

Consider each bit of information carefully. Try to determine what information is true and what information is false. Don't be fooled! Information you receive from other people, no matter who those persons are, may or may not be true. This means that the things you read in books, newspapers, and magazines and hear on TV or the radio may or may not be true, because <u>people</u> are responsible for all this information and <u>people are</u> <u>not perfect</u>.

STEP 5: Form your opinion.

Decide whether you are . . .

for,
against,
neither for nor against, or
undecided.

STEP 6: Continue to evaluate your opinion.

Keep an open mind. If you receive new information that proves your opinion is wrong, you need to change your opinion.

Changing your opinion may mean that it will become stronger or weaker, or that it will change into a new opinion completely.

No matter what your opinion is, you don't have to be afraid to change it if you discover new information that proves it to be wrong. Changing your opinion when you find you are wrong is a healthy, constructive thing to do.

69

So, it is important for you to remember that in order to form good opinions you will need to . . .

be aware of the information that you are receiving from your environmental influences,

keep an open mind,

gather information,

evaluate the information,

form your opinion, and

continue to evaluate your opinion.

If you form opinions without going through these six steps, you may find yourself pre-judging an issue.

What does it mean to pre-judge?

The next chapter will answer this question for you.

Chapter 4

When Opinions Become Prejudice

Pre-judging means that you judge an issue before you try to find out all the information about it. A person who pre-judges is often said to be prejudiced.

Because people's opinions affect the way they act, prejudice often leads to discrimination. Discrimination is treating another person unfairly because of a prejudice (a pre-judged opinion).

There are many kinds of prejudice. One kind is PHYSICAL PREJUDICE. Physical prejudice is pre-judging a person because of what the person looks like.

Physical prejudice often causes discrimination.

How do you think Aimee, Kevin, and David would feel if they knew they were not going to be invited to the party because some people thought they were ugly?

Are Aimee, Kevin, and David being treated fairly and honestly?

A second kind of prejudice is MENTAL PREJUDICE. Mental prejudice is pre-judging a person because of how smart the person is, how much the person knows, or how well the person thinks.

THIS NEW GAME LOOKS LIKE FUN, BUT WE NEED A FOURTH PERSON IF WE ARE GOING TO PLAY IT. WHO SHOULD WE GET?

FOR SURE WE DON'T WANT SHEILA! SHE'S IN THE LOWEST READING GROUP AT SCHOOL!

AT LEAST SHEILA IS NOT AS DUMB AS JUSTIN. JUSTIN FLUNKED THE SECOND GRADE.

Mental prejudice often causes discrimination.

How do you think Sheila and Justin would feel if they knew they were not going to be asked to play the new game because some people thought they were dumb?

Are Sheila and Justin being treated fairly and honestly?

A third kind of prejudice is SEXUAL PREJUDICE. Sexual prejudice is pre-judging people because they are male or female (boy or girl).

Sexual prejudice often causes discrimination.

How do you think John really feels about being left off the spelling team because he is a boy?

How do you think Kristy really feels about not being chosen for the baseball team because she is a girl?

Are John and Kristy treating each other fairly and honestly?

A fourth kind of prejudice is AGE PREJUDICE. Age prejudice is pre-judging people because of how old they are.

I'D SURE LIKE TO PLAY CARDS, BUT NOT WITH CHUCKIE AND GRANDPA. LITTLE KIDS ARE SO BABYISH THEY CAN'T DO ANYTHING RIGHT! AS FOR OLDER PEOPLE, THEIR BRAINS ARE SO WORN OUT THEY CAN'T THINK ANYMORE, AND OLD PEOPLE ARE ALWAYS SO SLOW!

Age prejudice often causes discrimination.

How do you think Grandpa and Chuckie would feel if they knew what Steve was thinking?

Are Grandpa and Chuckie being treated fairly and honestly?

A fifth kind of prejudice is RACIAL PREJUDICE. Racial prejudice is pre-judging people because they are Caucasian (white or brown), Mongoloid (Oriental), or Negroid (black).

WE DON'T WANT THAT CHINESE GUY ON OUR TEAM. THEY MAY BE SMART, BUT EVERYONE KNOWS THAT NONE OF THEM CAN PLAY SPORTS.

THE WHITE GUY IS TALL, BUT HE WON'T BE ABLE TO PLAY AS GOOD AS A BLACK PERSON.

Racial prejudice often causes discrimination.

How do you think the white boy really feels about being rejected because of his race?

How do you think the black boys would feel if they knew what the white boy was thinking?

Are the boys treating each other fairly and honestly?

A sixth kind of prejudice is NATIONAL PREJUDICE. National prejudice is pre-judging people because of where (what area or what country) they or their relatives come from.

National prejudice often causes discrimination.

How do you think Manuel would feel if he knew he was being rejected because he was Mexican-American?

Is Manuel being treated fairly and honestly?

A seventh kind of prejudice is **RELIGIOUS PREJUDICE.** Religious prejudice is pre-judging a person because of the person's beliefs about God and religion.

KEVIN, HOW ABOUT ME ASKING MY PARENTS IF YOU CAN SPEND THE WEEKEND AT MY HOUSE?

SURE DAVID! I'LL ASK MY PARENTS IF IT'S ALL RIGHT TO COME.

Religious prejudice often causes discrimination.

How do you think Kevin feels about David's parents not letting David be friends with him?

How do you think David feels about Kevin's parents not letting Kevin be friends with him?

Are David and Kevin being treated fairly and honestly?

An eighth kind of prejudice is POLITICAL PREJUDICE. Political prejudice is pre-judging a person because of the kind of government and laws the person would like to be a part of.

WHEN I PICKED MICHAEL UP FROM JOEL'S TODAY, I TALKED FOR A WHILE WITH HIS MOTHER. I COULDN'T BELIEVE MY EARS! DID YOU KNOW THAT SHE AND HER HUSBAND WANTED ADAMS TO BE PRESIDENT OF THE UNITED STATES?

THEY WANTED THAT JERK? THEY HAVE TO BE CRAZY TO VOTE FOR HIM!

Political prejudice often causes discrimination.

How do you think Joel would feel if he knew what Michael's mother was saying about his parents?

Are Joel and his parents being treated fairly and honestly?

A ninth kind of prejudice is SOCIAL PREJUDICE. Social prejudice is pre-judging a person because of what the person does, where the person lives, and what group of people the person spends most of his or her time with.

ARE YOU GOING TO INVITE HAROLD TO YOUR BIRTHDAY PARTY?

NO WAY! MY MOM SAYS THAT HE LIVES IN A PART OF TOWN WHERE THE POOR PEOPLE LIVE. DID YOU KNOW THAT HIS DAD IS A TRASH COLLECTOR?

Social prejudice often causes discrimination.

How do you think Harold would feel if he knew that he was not going to be invited to the birthday party because of where he lived and what his dad did for a living?

Is Harold being treated fairly and honestly?

A tenth kind of prejudice is ECONOMIC PREJUDICE. Economic prejudice is pre-judging a person because of how much money a person has or what he or she owns.

Economic prejudice often causes discrimination.

How do you think Nancy would feel if she knew she was not going to be asked to join the club because her family was poor?

Is Nancy being treated fairly and honestly?

Have you ever been pre-judged by another person because of . . .

the way you look,
how smart you are,
your being a male or female,
how old you are,
your being a certain race,
where you or your relatives came from,

what you believe about God and religion,

what kind of government and laws you would like to be
a part of,

what you do, where you live or who you spend most of
your time with, or

how much money you have or what you own?

Has another person's prejudice caused him or her to
discriminate against you?

If you have been discriminated against, how did it make you feel?

Do you ever pre-judge people because of . . .

the way they look,
how smart they are,
their being a male or female,
how old they are,
their being Caucasian, Oriental, or Negroid,
where they or their relatives come from,

what they believe about God and religion,

what kind of government and laws they would like
to be a part of,

what they do, where they live or what group of
people they spend most of their time with, or

how much money they have or what they own?

Has your prejudice caused you to discriminate?

If you have discriminated against another person, how do you think
that person felt?

When a person is prejudiced, he is being unfair to himself and the issue he or she is considering.

Thus, it's important to avoid pre-judging issues.

Conclusion

You have many opinions about many issues. The opinions you have
are either . . .

NO MATTER WHAT YOUR OPINIONS ARE THERE ARE TWO IMPORTANT THINGS TO REMEMBER:

1. WHATEVER YOUR OPINIONS ARE RIGHT NOW, THEY CAN CHANGE.
2. YOUR OPINIONS AFFECT THE WAY YOU ACT.

The people, places, and experiences (environmental influences) in your life affect the opinions you form.

What you do with the information you receive from your environment is up to you.

To form a good opinion remember to . . .

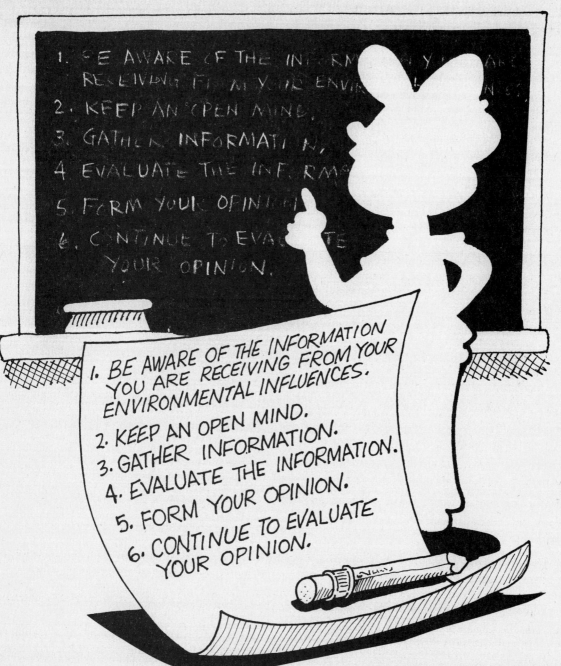

If you form opinions without going through these six steps, you may find yourself pre-judging an issue.

When a person pre-judges an issue, he or she often becomes prejudiced.

Prejudice, whether it is . . .

physical,

mental,

sexual,

age,

racial,

national,

religious,

political,

social, or

economic . . .

can cause discrimination.

Discrimination is often cruel and unfair and can be harmful to every person involved.

This is why you must form each and every one of your opinions very carefully and do your best to . . .